CSU Poetry Series XXXI

Beckian Fritz Goldberg

BODY BETRAYER

Cleveland State University Poetry Center

ACKNOWLEDGEMENTS

THE AMERICAN POETRY REVIEW: "L'Age Mûr"

THE ANTIOCH REVIEW: "Spring." Copyright 1983 by The Antioch Review, Inc. First appeared in the *The Antioch Review,* Vol. 41, No. 2 (Spring 1983). Reprinted by permission of the editors.

THE CONTEMPORARY REVIEW: "The Flamingo at the Palo Verde Nuclear Plant"

CRAZYHORSE: "Horses at Estero Beach," "Nightgowns," "Visiting the Stockyards"

CUTBANK: "Refraction"

THE GETTYSBURG REVIEW: "Desert Winter" and "She Comes to My Door" are reprinted, by permission of the editors, from *The Gettysburg Review* (Winter 1989).

HAYDEN'S FERRY REVIEW: "Bad Sleep," "First Crazy," "Keeping Warm in New York," "Paris," "Salvation"

NIMROD: "Cutting Worms," "Emerson's Walk to a Shaker Village"

THE NORTH AMERICAN REVIEW: "Hartford County"

POETRY NORTHWEST: "Balconies," "Birdscaping," "The Cloud by Desire," "Fable: The Woman and the Iris," "Geraniums," "Revolution," "Slow Dancing," "What We Do in the Evening"

QUARTERLY WEST: "Walking in the Solstice"

THE SENECA REVIEW: "Cranes," "Trajectory"

TENDRIL: "The Consolation of Celibacy," "The Perception of Motion," "State Street Motel"

THE VIRGINIA QUARTERLY REVIEW: "First Love"

ISBN 0-914946-82-X
    0-914946-83-8 (paperback)

Library of Congress catalog number: 90-83469

Funded Through
Ohio Arts Council

727 East Main Street
Columbus, Ohio 43205-1796
(614) 466-2613

CONTENTS

IV

**for my mother and father
and for Dick**

*And what is full of dread
Dreams within the heart—for look,
We expect most from what we fear.*

—Kenneth Patchen

It loves to happen.

—Euripides

I

REVOLUTION

Like the curve of the body
that rises only in sleep,
light in November. I unwrapped the bells
of new wine glasses tucked with tissue paper,
folds of great worry smoothing
to the floor. Behind me in the window
the tiger eye of autumn. I could
smell the visitors coming with fruit baskets
and scribbles of violets.
And then the glasses were standing
in a clear row, so it remained
only for a small transparent man to walk
his crystal spaniel along that boulevard.
I was, for a moment, almost a sphere.
Then the sour streak of your mouth
cursing the way I kept a house.
And a sheet tented the floor,
a remnant shade of some dream
last night, crease like an orchid.

What a man can say now
to a woman he loved this morning
is like finding the earth revolves
around a fly. Tonight the edges
of me part and float like brides,
like ghosts, one in the piano bar
on the late show, one drowsing over the cool
fringe of the cat, one in some other year
where the schoolyard is whiskered with frost,
the pink moth glowing
huge on the east wall . . .

I have heard of countries where revolution
has broken out over an old broom,
its hairshock of silence. Where heads

come off because the moon dizzies
in the shoemaker's wine.

It is too much for one body.
Lying down as darkness sheets
the eye violet. Waking in the morning
with the sadness
of opening a gift alone.

THE MINISTER'S WIFE ADDRESSES THE GARDEN

This morning speech is glitter while she dreams
them naked, and the shin and the leaf of the citrus
shining. Black spiderlegs of hair swirl around
the aureoles of Adam in the front row, the mole
low on Eve's hip spoiling the curve the way a city
far off in the desert does, and the chestnut tuft
filigrees beneath smile lines a cousin's thighs
have pressed in silk and the tea roses are burning
like the boy's peeled scab, the woman's ring finger
missing the ring. She knows it's late in the world
but it is all temptation, all comfort,
like a house where you wake to the scent of cinnamon
and go searching.

She loves the way shadow comes and holds them
in places unnameable and lonely, the bellies of old women
and the buttocks of old men and the pink-rimmed
tips of young boys. And if they have fallen
they have fallen in a light that renders all other things
relative and slow, strips small comet tails from the points
of berries, tests red punch in the bowl like Host.
She'll wait for the man to rise, covering himself,
and the woman clutching her breasts as if, suddenly,
they were to begin again. It's as if the flesh
of flowers, the rover mums and iris, could conceive
they are not all flower, but something

that dies with the flower just the same. Take the sinner,
the one the women whispered to her. One
who made his seed fall into his wife's purse when
she was buried. Take the widower who discovers
nakedness like this and morning marigolds
with their bird-pulse of red, and the quick of air
in fence slats, and the locust skin,
dry, hanging in the slivers like ghost honey, while she
loses her place, dreams of unbuttoning slowly,
saving him, the flesh white, white as the heat in grief.

GERANIUMS

My husband does Jolson in the kitchen.
My father-in-law at 81 has taken up
telling dirty jokes—interrupts
to tell them, or to mention did we know
most people die in March. But today
he stands in the garden he built
complete with ceramic frogs in pools, and talks
about sperm, how marvelous it is.
That each time a man ejaculates he releases
thousands, and out of those thousands
in a thousand times, one
makes it. Nearly blind in one eye,
diabetic, his balance cloudy, he leans
against the planter and says
what a miracle of odds it is
to be born. Squints out at the sky.
My husband croons *rockabye* from the kitchen.
The trumpet flowers suck at his father's white sleeve.
She always makes me get dressed up, he says.
But where the hell am I going?
We sit. And the light just stays
the way it always would if we could make it.
Over the pink geraniums
a bee sounds like thousands.
I breathe the pony odor of peat,
a trace of chlorine. Watch
the way the water
returns through the clay frog's lips
and jiggles the sky. Think
of the odds against this . . .

ELEGY FOR THE GIANTS

1. *Radiance*

I stand in the kitchen
speaking to an open cupboard
softly, as if there the spirit
of a loved one settled, a rose-bordered
dish. Grief when it is new
stones the brain with radiance.
The candle bounces
its wide brilliance, an upended
skirt in the landscape of the wall
like one woman sucked in
though the whole snow is still.
Her husband sits in the same chair
muttering, *I'm just an old bag of shit.*
Her grown son lifts the crystal lids
of candy dishes and stares in
their clear mouths. Later
beneath her bras and scarves
we find wishbones. And in the tender
cotton of boxes earrings or
a brooch once traveled in. Wishbones.
Pure like the open arms of stickmen.
And gray and yellow and clean. I don't know
as we search what we are searching
for, our hands stretched, running on air.

2. *Vigil*

That morning the tongue lay black violet
swollen like a small dome. Her breath

shallow and so even, even
like no wave but the one

a finger might leave
in dry sugar, the blank

white things we can't help
but touch. That is,

being human. We separate
even in our dreams and watch

ourselves walking
corridors clean as sweat

or stabbed—red beads
of blood swarming the slit

like ants a crack—stabbed
by a stranger

who is also us. In the dream
her tongue burned by the oxygen

thrusts like a lizard.
It is not a thing you can forgive,

the way the body of an old woman
lies uncovered, the silver hairs,

one nipple staring off
like a lazy eye, and nurses white

as unlit candles clustered down
the hall. She opens her eyes

and sees only her own kitchen,
cobwebs, shelves, and tells me,

dust.

3. *The Giants*

We are born with the heads of giants.
If you magnify newborns
in their true proportions they look
like monsters, their heads huge, their eyes
Jupiters. Even the featherless
young wrens fall topheavy from nests,
eyes closed, bulging and dark
as bloodblisters. They fall like
loose thumbs stuck in plums. Somehow
we know this has to do

with everything, the body
betrayer. For days, we talk
as if she will come back. As if
some black telephone has failed us.
After months, even this is gone.
There is only strangeness, each morning
I find a bowl of wine in the heel
of my sock. This is absence.
No last words, no bits
of wisdom, no famous accomplishments
I can list for her life. Only
a note in a mileage record
from a summer they crossed the country,
Today I saw my first wild daffodils.
Only a clean house, a long marriage,
and a beautiful son. The days,
the days murmur sweet things
they don't mean. The sun is only
a white pin worn by a pebble
on a grave. But we are born
with the heads of giants.
And we remember.

                    —*in memory of Lily Goldberg*

THE MOTHER KNIFE

for my mother

The face, the face with no nose
is the front of a house
shrunken—the door's
taut little mouth, the lidless
windows closer together. I make my mother
drive by three times. Nervy the last time,
she turns around in the driveway. No one
is home. They have painted the sills
green. Heartless. On the porch a rag's
dried curled over the back of a chair.
I look into the air for myself like the dead,
or dying. Myself with a strip
of green willow. Hard to interpret
some thirty years gone. Like a drink
stops fizzing. Or a rag
scabs over where it's left. Ordinary
like that, but strange
darkness at the windows as if
each room inside was out, each
a hand in a sock. I want to rush
in and get it all straight, my beginning.
Sit again in the kitchen enormous
with summer, aware of nothing
but dust nervous in a shaft of light, ripe
tomatoes smiling wide open
beneath my mother's knife. But she
has turned with me
down the road, house sinking, fields low
with this year's drought. Life is easy,
it just goes. Goes far, no matter what
we do, into its routine distance. Hand
into sock until it finds no hole.

THE CHILDREN DREAM DEATH

The boy is sitting in the closet cutting off
the heads of dolls to send back to Russia.
His mother's in the kitchen licking the backs
of stamps which gleam like fever. This is how
it begins. In the window of his bedroom
a garbage truck drives up and the men grab
his parents and stuff them in. The devil,
red tail crooked with the poise
of a phonograph arm, hisses, *If you tell,*
if you tell . . . The next evening at the table
his mother says, What's wrong with him.
He doesn't eat. He begins to cry and confesses
everything, the dolls and the truck and
the garbage and the devil. All night
he trembles for them to come.

It is midnight and the girl
shops with her mother. They load the cart
with packages of frozen broccoli, corn,
and next is her father lying peacefully
in the shredding wings of frost above
the freezer case. The tips of his brown shoes
sugared with ice. His arms folded.
She cries to her mother, Look, look,
then the furniture and the silence
the nightlight in the hallway come see.

The house is familiar but wrong.
The boy's mother is saying, It's time. We
were told to pack our toothbrushes.
His father says, Now we'll be leaving.
There's yellow carpet in the doorway
like bad light. They're dressed for a day
on the patio, a trip to the bank.
It's time, they say. We'll just

take our toothbrushes and be
going. He can't stop them
because they are so simple. He wakes up
and the moon floats its blank head
over roofs in the darkness which does not
speak English, though it has lived here.

SHE COMES TO MY DOOR

with the fervor of a Witness,
tells me of the strange case
in Santa Ana where the woman burned
but not the book she was reading,
and of the man who went up
in his Chevy like a sun god
but the wheel cool. There is no science

to explain this fire, no faith
to stop it. As far back as China goes,
for example, there are stories
of peasant boys going off like rockets
suddenly though no one
had touched them. In a halo
like the heart has

the body would combust. I do not
tell her this. I do not offer
my theory that there is nothing
reasonable about the lives we get
and too late
desire. She hands me literature

and the xerox black photographs:
A man, the shape of a man, who flared
from his shoes and his armchair
one night while they stayed perfect.
There was no oven lit, no lamp,
no secret oxygen to satisfy
this fury. Only beings from another place

she says, could do this. And I smile,
she smiles, when I say I believe her.
I believe the girl I was comes back

when, sometimes, I touch her old books. This
is the fire that catches. Memory

terrible as lust. I give the girl at my door
her photographs and shut myself
back in. She knocks at the next house.
There is a long silence
inside that turns slowly.
We know who we are.

SURVIVAL TOWN

Just up the road from Mercury past the *No Trespassing*
you can still find remains of the pigs we blew
in '57. The craters had fallen like blue sacks
open in the early light. We knew everything by then,
how the shirtbacks of colonels grieved sweat,
the scientists' seraphs from Lucky Strikes cooled,
the windows of Vegas womanly trembled. So we
dumped them on the Flats good distances apart
saluting as we left and they stood stiff
in the uniforms the tailors had made them
grunting, What the hell are we doing here. Let's
see if there's anything to eat. On the way back
we passed the ashes of the town we'd built
and blasted to shit one spring. When it was new
I used to watch the windows of its houses bleed
like a little dye in the evening, its power lines
tie darkness to the empty offices, to the fallout shelters,
to the houses again. I'd imagine in each kitchen,
coffee, beer, potatoes. In each, a woman mopping
the floor with her high heels on. It was a kind of home.
Then we laid the mannequins around and left them,
Priscillas and Johns in bedrooms, their legs
twined, or the women on top, or the men's heads
buried in a plastic twat murmuring, Let's
try it a way we've never done it.
It was ecstasy city, but we blew it
the way we blew everything, the pink
skin of pigs that was almost human,
the clothes that covered its nakedness like ours,
the hollow torsos of redheads who never got it
so the Russians, the Chinese, the aliens in silver ships
wouldn't get it either, even if they laid
down their arms among us, their bodies burning
for one another in the wild sodomies
of everything and light.

THE ROAD OF LOST CLOTHES

As if each row of the flooded alfalfa field was struck
as the car slowed, the water shimmied and flashed down
moon. Nutmeat dampness seemed to sleepwalk
the rank frill of air from the sugar beet factory
its towers lit out there, she'd think, like the first
City of the Future. She'd stare at it with some boy
or just a cigarette, each leg cocksure and cool
up against the dash. She needed time then
and space and this was just about where
they'd happen, out Stapley Road, onto the thin-tarred
one laner toward Guadalupe. She could hear crickets
as they drilled into their jewel: After ages
only a slight nick. It was hard hearted

black she liked, no horizon, that nothing
but a taillight from a trucker or a cat eye catching it
would glow against. Sometimes on the way there
or returning, she'd meet a single half-laced shoe
or a whole gray shirt pooling itself on the road
and wonder who could go far without his shirt and who
could have had so little time for his shoe he couldn't
come back . . . Until the night a man from the fields

loved her, slid his hand slowly through the dark ages,
the enlightenment, the fissionable new centuries
under her dress and sighed there
at that point where they knew the world
would end, and them only halfway there
but far enough, unbuttoned, unbuckled, a strap down
into the abundance of darkness on a back seat
for her to see a man's shirt when it slides down
goes backwards through all the stages of caress.
A woman's mantis-like first step out of her yellow skirt
is always into the center of that road.

THE PERCEPTION OF MOTION

First he dropped two iron balls,
the light one and the heavy one,

from the tower, at the same instant.
A pigeon went on overhead

chintzed with light.
He did not have to wait long:

A peasant rolling a wagon wheel
down the stone street

let it go ahead of him
and part two priests

walking from the baptistery, their cassocks
rising about the height of the chickens.

Then the wind dropped.
The wheel fell against a nut merchant's stall.

The balls clacked
on the ground like two beads,

one sound. He carried them home
and wrote, *two round objects*

of different weight will fall
at the same speed, straight.

But it was hard to describe
as that moment for the peasant

when the quail shot in flight
shuddered and moved back

and dropped in an arc
behind him

reddening the field grass.
Each word reflects belief

about the motion
it stops. This was most difficult

for the priests
who held Galileo *heretic*

yet could not deny
such a being

moved forward as he fell—
just as the spring water that year,

in Pisa, received its impetus
from river ice

that had carried it slowly
toward release.

The peasant, Giorgio, the vine-tiller
who could not write

would have told them
there were tiny animals of God

in wine, that tunneled
like ticks into his red feet,

but he was lucky.
That year, as any other,

snow fell, the dog's teeth
knew the plush of quails' necks . . .

Sometimes he missed
and all the field birds rose

at once, in the same direction,
and revolved.

It was hard to explain the good
of the invisible;

as talking to his daughter at night
he thought of many things

but only told her one.

II

SALVATION

A helicopter's shadow pinwheels
on the canyon floor. Wild burros
are inclining just the distance from one another
friends do, when presence
but not touch
is the right consolation. Surely

there is a reason these things
make a world: The Colorado curves
the famous textbook set of parallel lines
that will meet at infinity.
As we watch from the rim
a silver beating in the dry grasses,
the halo of the chopper's descent,
all space changes like the nap of velvet.

Through binoculars we read
the mouths of burros
who must be calling out something
it took them a long time to learn.
Airlifted above the rest, one
hangs calmly in harness, bobs his head
slowly as if to say yes, yes . . .

We know the story of Icarus is not true.
Dumbest damn creatures, the ranger says.
Don't even look up.
They pay no attention to the mother copter
bearing the gray burro from point A
over the lips of the mesas, up
toward the white cattle trucks
clustered at point B. They remain

bent to the weeds
that burst in rock, medieval alchemists
hard at study, while in the air
the genius of them makes
a new assumption. This morning
one by one they discover
the coming of an age.

Yet even as they are moved they forget
and, miles away on new plateaus,
will resume their old beliefs
in the magic of fissures, in the luck
of the foot, in scent the bridegroom
hesitating
at the hollow of the scented . . .

Already they recall only distantly
rising in harness,
as we do falling in dreams,
staring out as the trucks rock
down Highway 66
their eyes holding
the kind of picture we have
when we are not ourselves.

PARIS

That summer my brother worked nights
in geriatrics. Sometimes he had to pull
the shit right out of their bowels, frantic,
dry, afraid to waste anything.

The really sick did not even dream
of going home. Ethel dreamed of Paris
and was released, late December.
Wearing a deadly shade of lipstick
she made her son drive three times past
a poster of the Eiffel Tower
in an airline window, went
into his bathroom and drank cleaning fluid.

The fence around the hospital
had a crack running like a ziggurat.
He'd take their vital signs and drink
Jack Daniels on a bench. When he stumbled
onto the floor singing, "All of me,
why not take—" he was fired.

He thought a while of doing something else.
Of going away and seeing the world.
Africa. Women in New York.
But they took him back;
they had no one else.

He learned the odor of a mattress
one of them had died on
was vast. But in three months
he'd only fainted twice. He'd let it slump
over the window ledge, stained
with brown continents. And about four
in the morning when the smell receded,

when the air was spreading
blotter ink blue, every morning
until the thirty-first of August,
he and the fat woman
would sit by the window watching the black
backs of the pecan leaves
shake once in the wind, and she
would turn to him
and whisper, "See the lion?"

BAD SLEEP

Everyone has a version. The sailing ship
becomes stranded in seaweed and holds
still for days. The passengers
drink up all the liquor, stare angles in the air
like cut glass. Probably, the woman says, they think
I've been captured by Spaniards. Probably,
says the fellow in beige, my wife's gone off
with the kid in leather underwear. At night
the mist opaques like a dead woman
in her honeymoon picture. Seaweed chokes
portholes, wood planks begin to sweat.
Their sleep is restless because they have told
all their secrets to kill time and still
they are here. The captain's hoarding rum.
Suddenly the seaweed twitters like skylarks.
Its pink fever flowers. Probably, the cigar man
says, this is the end of the world. He mourns
the brief beauty of television offers, the moustache,
the blue blazer, the man seated at the grand
piano in firelight offering excerpts
of every great symphony ever written
on a two record set. The spinster says,
Now my sister will be setting the table . . .
They stand on deck gazing where there's only
deep blue between the weeds like panes.
They have nothing to do.
It goes like this: Now my sister is laying
down the knives. My wife, sighs one, is watching
the well of his boot as he undresses. My father,
says the woman, is dialing the Spanish Embassy.
And so it pours. My son is shooting
snails with his BB gun in the garden, my lover
is changing the furniture, my cat is running off
with a pack to the dump, my mother is returning

from her honeymoon with blurred
snapshots, the snapshots loosening from
their dry glue and shuffling in the dark pages
the faces of lost twins and half-wits from
the other side, and the seaweed's saying, I'm wild
about everything, honey. You could wrap me around
your little finger. And on mantelpieces
the dead in their photographs echo this
and hang around on the shore holding still, each
with his tiny boat out there, suspended,
digging light like the demon spades of leaves.

FIRST CRAZY

As if a rock threw itself down from a tree.
The stick took hold of the girl,
made her hush it hard in the soft dirt
of the bank. She crouched and wiped the line
away with her hand, as if the halved
apple grew back together. She would try
to walk away. But something had her.
And she'd rake the same line in the same
place. Crouch, heal with her hand.
Even at that age, we knew. We called
softly, *Barbara, Barbara,* coaxing her
from the canal's edge to the house which

spring grass tickled to itself like a magnet.
There, in the kitchen stood Barbara glowing
strange as a bulb left on in the daylight,
word after word shorting her, *Yes, no—
wait—I have to—no—I—yes. Wait—*
until my mother quietly closed a door
and dialed the phone and my father
drove her to her father alone, and she
disappeared from afternoons, school.
As if space flew the bird.

I thought at first it was because I'd told her
what I'd heard, how women bleed.
But later, years later, I heard she lived
in Cordes Junction married to a drummer
and glazing pottery, reds and blues dividing
from the cream of her hand. By then the world
loved only to happen: Grandmothers stickpinned
their shades to the sills and burned
birds' nests on the stove. Men emptied guns
into their televisions. The whole country yearned
to float bombs among the stars.

And somehow it all seemed normal until this
evening, sun fermenting low and peach hair shadows
along the street, a blonde girl
walking one foot on, one foot off
the curb beside her house. Losing and coming
back for, over and over, a loose pink ballet slipper
which flapped from her heel like a mouth.
As if speech were letting itself out
the back way, slowly, from our lives.

TRAJECTORY

for Thomas James

I read your poems. The blast
in my mouth like water
I can't swallow. The warm
rooms of the day are shut.
My window looks out over a piece

of evening, piece of sharp lead.
I am having my own doubts
about creation. This is an ordinary house
where change persists.
My shadow falls on uneaten bread,
the seasons cripple themselves
like women who begin
their intimacies with pain.
This is all that goes on. Not one
of your one hundred passion plays
lives. Not the one

where the blood burst
like a small primrose above your ear.

Not the one where your floor must stare
up the eye-socket black sleeve
of your coat. But who knew

what living was? Something
that flew and ate and breathed beside us
long enough. Like sleep, a space we never fill,

or the lily-blankness of a florist's hands
which beckoned us once a year. This is

one other night. The air bruises with approach.
Strange things live on
the soft mold of lamentation—a lamp
in a field of ash, water glass
and paper. And when I see
your name in small black hammers
on a page, it seems
somehow permanent
as the thought of sky
in a blind bird.

THE FLAMINGO AT THE PALO VERDE
NUCLEAR PLANT

Who can say how
the lost get as far as they do. Suddenly
above the waste water lake his current
softened with forgiveness. The guys on break
shook their heads and grinned.
It was almost like before a holiday

when work goes easily, the hand half-in
another life. There was a gathering:
a few reporters, the foreman, a secretary
from the Audubon. The water flocked with light.

The bird strolled then, corsage on stilts. Or
a model on the beach, striking
each pose for a long time, long enough
to think what to do first
in the New World . . .

Helicopters swiped their arcs
in the air, dropped cargo nets and dragged
nothing, intersected and abstract
as plans for grief.
Slivering his blush wings
to his black tailfeathers, he found
their margin of error, crossed
the length of the water
over and over

with the new evening. It was almost
a ballet. Or who could say
what. When I was a kid it was jackrabbits
standing up in traffic
like someone called them. As always

no one expected a history of this.
The flamingo lighting with his wings
kept open could have been saying
grace, while the men whispered *son-of-a-bitch*
and *how'd he get here* . . .
feeling a bit sorry, but perfect, as one does

about a thing that has to be done.

NIGHTGOWNS

The curve of every river is beautiful.
Black houses fold like jersey along the street.
It is still a kingdom
when all your neighbors are asleep,
even your husband, and you can smoke.
What else is there to wait for?
I'm almost thirty before I notice
my mother can't stop buying nightgowns,
must have forests, rivers
of tricot and cotton and bird-designs
hidden in ordinary closets—even one
from a white sale where a leopard's face
is cut off below the nose, his mouth
hemmed up. A real mistake.
I hear the neighbor's garden hose
running tonight, water that can't heal.
A retired engineer, he is asleep
while the St. Augustine drowns.
In the moon the summer bugs zip open
tiny wakes on his black water. Alone,
with his bleached trees, like movie blondes
whispering *darling*, his lawn rises.
This wind pulls like elastic. Somewhere gazelles

swing like empty hangers, if you watch them
from a distance. A woman imagines what she can.
I wish there were an all night department store,
an insomniac's garden. Nothing too wild:
The lingerie hanging like ghosts,
ivory slippers poised to walk in forever.
Once, she took me with her.
We tried all the black lace before mirrors
on Saturday morning, the salesgirls frowning,
my father somewhere ambling
to his friend the doctor's house
and finding him a suicide. A red slash.

At night, when she takes them and slips them on, where
does she think she is going. Nowhere in the heartland
is beautiful. A pipe whines down
the side of my neighbor's house and the flooded lawn
rises. Gray water braids in the curb
along the sidewalk. The engineer is dreaming
there's a dark girl in the plumbing. He's building
a lagoon. There, the flowers float tenderly
as the shadows of price tags on store carpets.
Mother, there's night inside the body all the time.

SEVEN

In the last nights
he wanted ice. His voice
would rise and step
into our sleep like a cat.
Its eyes glowed.

How easily morning came,
the glass of water
on the nightstand, warm,
watching a disk
on the ceiling.

He used to cry, *You
are the fruit of my loins.*
Came from a time and a place
where people actually
said such things.

My husband carried him
out over the threshhold
of the kitchen. Father
like a child of bones.
I wrote his name
in his clothes, taped
his name to each thing—
the gambler's hat,
the flashlight. The china cup
his mother had filled with wine
for Elijah. These things.

In the flower beds, tired
old galaxies of alyssum,
the frost-bleached ferns, dragged
light flaking from the urns

he'd placed there with his
own hands. But houses
do not remember or forget.
It is as if they were never awake.

Now, in my house
the candle's blue eye hunts
for seven days. The clothes
lie in a box, tongue-tied.
The cup
huddles all to itself
in a cupboard.

Who will find it again
someday and carry
it away. Easily,
like a vowel or a rose.

WHAT WE DO IN THE EVENING

Sometimes it is discovering a new virus
that makes men explode, and not selling it
to anyone. Sometimes it's believing
rumors that in the last house on the street
a man drinks the blood of strays, women whose
nightgowns insinuate beyond the fringes of
bermuda lawns. It is seeing something strange
and being sad for it, like the wizened twin
born with claws and a slow trapezoid of a head,
whom the nurse pities and raises secretly. On my street
it was the old couple, their weeds fermenting

all summer till pollen swizzled in the yard,
curtains sucked the glass. It was her pale brow,
his hair slicked back like death, the white
neckbrace she wore to the All-Nite Mart
as if her head were serenely planted on
a dish. We knew what marks it hid. Then
it had not occurred to us how strange—and therefore
sad—it must be to live forever, homesick
for dusks when she-wolves prickled and
nightbirds swooned the branch before they
touched. It must have spoiled everything,

the invention of electricity, the dayglow
like virgins lasting through the night, and
heartache to wake among the first stars for
the million-and-seventeenth time and say, Dear,
what shall we do this evening, then wander again
the clean cemetery under the freeway, crushing
plastic roses underfoot. For a while
it was happiness to know the shy undead
dwelled at the end of Matlock Street, that
somewhere a twin grew with one wish,
to find his brother's perfect body

and possess it. Desire had always lived
like this—a man eats spiders when nothing else
creeps across his lips. Tonight is the full moon,
houses set back along the street as if
waiting for the first to come forward and
confess. But what a house would confess
is nothing: A door swings in it, an oven
hates everything it sees. It's the invention
of houses themselves that seems strange, their heads
dim triangles the shadows speak to like sisters,
their shrunken hands in windows that dinner guests

mistake for a cypress, a bogeyman, a bat. Sometimes
it is seeing the yellow room thrown out
by lampsilk to the nails of the grass when
you are suddenly hungry at midnight and next door
the retired colonel in wrinkled undershorts is
pouring a Scotch neat and talking down
to his Great Dane who studies him as if this

will be on the test. Let's drink to anything,
he says. Let's live to infinity and never
tell anyone. Mostly, it is just this,
watching in secret and making up the words,
a fluorescent lining up the worried
brow of the dog while a man lifts his glass
and the glass lifts the color of him
in the window—as if he knows I'm out there
possessing him, the bird's-blood
of small shadows crossing me, the dog, him,
in common, briefly. The beautiful undead.

SLOW DANCING

Moving, our feet
imagine the dimensions
of a box. A clarinet
streaks the room. We sway
in time and out. This
maybe this
is the only way to live.

Mornings my father,
soloist, rises on his arms
leans like E-flat
into the sweet bar of his walker.
His legs dangle
just like marionettes.
Maybe this

is what our grandmothers called
slow dancing, the way
I'd like to bear him up
waltz on top
like I did as a girl, barefoot,
standing on his brown shoes.
We worked then
just like a mirror.

And who could know
that this
would happen, crumpling
the way the long notes do
eventually. The poor trumpeters
putting their whole mouths
on the air.

The air not moving.

THE CONSOLATION OF CELIBACY

So cold that morning, not a fly in the air.

Our friend the ex-priest can't stop talking
about the disembowelled ones the boy Alvaro
led him to. Women nursed their children
outside the shacks, pulled
sweaters that would not stretch across their breasts.
He drinks gin with dinner, and it's satisfying
the way each guest has stopped listening and sits
toward Colombia, but is really thinking
about some day or night he loves.
Maybe, Father, memory's the right punishment—
When I close my eyes the old house grows up
the way legs in a running dream go on and on.
Make up a reason: You're married to God and you wear
black skirts. My sister and I used to wonder
who owns the body, the man with the breasts of the woman,
the woman with the hair of the man.
We used to watch white June moths doubling mid-air
in the alleys. "They can't help it," we whispered
and closed our eyes letting it go on, on
like almost all the girls we'd talked to
who were convinced they'd *never.*
And, in a way, we never did. Remember
our smooth stomachs and calves dripping solitary
from early summer baths. Nights
we climbed into like booths where we kneeled
undressed, down to the damp lace of our thoughts.
"I'm going to be a nun," my sister said. Three months later
she smelled like him, said, "I think about Saint Teresa
when we're doing it." I picture her
telling a priest in the dim Chicago parish that she was
tired after twenty years, forgiving him. Her hands
clutch a comb and a kleenex in her open purse

as if she's not quite sure which she needs.
And all the time the priest is thinking of a green
watercolor behind the house he grew up in. A certain squirrel.
So cold that morning. I remember
what it feels like to be just one, clean as a bead
or a new orange—just like I remember the story
lovemaking makes up, want to
remember the one about the monk who ravishes
brown women with flakes of milk on their breasts.
They took off his skin, slowly. He was talking
to the pair of lips we all imagine in the air, praying
for convergence. He raised his eyes a little to see
everything coming back: It is dinner. Strangely,
the ex-priest is saying, as he stepped over
the blue-red parts of the body—while the boy watched,
his mouth open—he blessed them.

III

CUTTING WORMS

As all children, he learned of it—
this strange ability to receive the cut

and go on living like two
worms shrugging across the soil.

This delighted him. The self
was endless and he proved it

slicing the earthworm
gray as a laboratory liver.

How odd it was
a brain without location

like God, or Joseph the accountant's son
when his heart stopped,

who became two Josephs, one cool
as his finger in mud

one still dancing on top of his bicycle,
grinning.

The grin the worm wears
is its whole body

flexing over lantana roots,
quartz grains like grooved roads.

When it is severed
with a spade or a jackknife

it rolls and glistens and becomes
them, two worms parting from

a point in the dust
as if they agreed to it.

They are not capable of pain,
they are like girls' ribbons

or the saints whose greatest virtue
his teacher said

was to be disinterested.
He understood

the soul was like this,
not in any part

and so dumb
that you could shred a man

with a razor blade
as leaves' shadows sometimes slit open

on his face, and never find it.
He was not after it:

He would sometimes halve a worm
on the chair of a swing

to show the others
and give the new pair

names, and wonder
if they ever met again

and knit like true skin,
slick and whole as grace.

He could not imagine it
any other way.

EMERSON'S WALK TO A SHAKER VILLAGE

The heat of summer came
like a wound from a friend. Spiders
touched a web to a thornbush
by the gate, and tiny shadows pooled underneath
the gentians. He wrote, *the days of September
saturate*, and walked
past the shiftless pig farms, 20 miles, to Stow

then Ashburnam. All night he'd felt the reach
of sweat. Now he was far,
a whole day's walk. His house, that nothing,
like a seashell far inland
was always settling. That morning
while the good Sisters readied breakfast

the Brethren gave an honest account
of their faith. Cloutman showed him
the vineyard, the orchard, the herb-room.
The grapes were both white and Isabella,
the orchard dumb with shape. He thought,
this capitalist is old and never dies.

In that shade he felt his father's hand
on his neck, forcing him into the water
off some wharf or bathhouse,
and wanted to hide as he used to
in Aunt Mary's prayers.
He liked to imagine her mind,

its infinite Himalayan folds.
He told his friends, the world
is awakening to union
like a crocus under snow. And that day
if Hawthorne had not been inclined to pontificate,

and he himself with a cold, and if
they could have stayed 24 hours
he might have convinced

the Shaker farmers to awake, to propagate.
They showed humor.
They appeared to understand
the idea of union, the second crop.

HARTFORD COUNTY

Old man Christiansen tied the newborns
in a feedsack, set it down, moving
just like a body, no arms, no legs. Alive
like the magic sack in a fairy tale.
Then the farmer, or his oldest son, put them mewing
to the water—the worst moment, the moment before
they went down in that darkness hot
as breath, the last pricked seam of light their claws
pinpointed in the burlap. Drowning them
was quick. The water widened and widened,
blinked the rust edges of the trough
as if amazed. Air rained up. Nothing else
changed for miles: The barn door blind
with its seethe of dung and hay, the wheatfield
brushed backward, the chickens tipping
to seed. It was kindness; so many were born
each season. My father, my brothers,
stood over the water, waiting.
The cat strolled its eight spare lives
through shadow and stinkweed. Where I came from
people were used to the way
chickens jigged without their heads, assumed
the hog and the lamb had understood
their brief lives. And lived theirs
like death, making room for something. Always
called the Gill boy crushed beneath the tractor
angel. Harvested their fields, and saw all winter
a foot more of numb Wisconsin sky.

CRANES

fit the water at their narrowest
points—the perfect bar of fractions is light,
restless, flashes along the end of gray lake.
It splits them   in half. On the water they see cranes
flat   the sequence
of the current swelling through them
pinching them into crests, spilling them
like slow gloss of egg white   back
into cranes. Each bird with his strange code
of shape stands and lets the sun print him

nervously on a blue glaze. All the weight of cranes
evaporates   like the weight of a house
in memory: Heaviness beside it, the weather
and the wish to   bend is a kind of movement
it takes on. If we understood

our peripheries, our cells   have a life that is not
in them, weightless   like something that water could
be interested in

we might not hold   except as tallness holds
marsh grass. The water stares cranes . . .
as in the mind we hold there
and somewhere   apart.

Our living is not about our living. Still birds
divide a light. Their heartbeat perches
on water. For a moment they are not
cranes but the persistence of something that
stalls   on the lake like their name. Moment

weeps like a bullfrog. Each gray
breast is shuffled by the wind. In the house
oh house   the mirrors move.

VISITING THE STOCKYARDS

Behind the splitrail fence, a few bulls step
crushing shadows into their own manure.
Our white hands curve neatly over the rails.
They are surrounded. The teachers lean in red sweaters
near a gate, and over us
the cattle's voice breaks, ragged
and in great hunks. It's May
and the foreman leads us slowly toward
the crusted walls of two barns, lit
by a break in the clouds like a small village
under a dome of glass.
In the bulls' eyes it is always night.
Kept for breeding, he says, they
grow heavy gazes in front of us
like stonewort blooming in deep ponds.
This morning men wear gloves like oven mitts
and herd a brown steer from the mud,
past a metal gate, into a corridor,
and other men wait, dressed in bloody smocks.
When the blade flashes in the stall,
its cud pours out like milk, full of slivers.
Over the hills there's a little cache of rain.
Its legs fold twice: the knees bend
and hesitate, as if from some sudden
recollection, then crush on the floor.
Some of the young girls
have shut their eyes, but over the hills
the sky's a sheer nightgown
showing the flesh where darkness
has set its tiny seam. And, in their yard,
the heifers pull slowly apart
staring at something else
vacant, like new widows
with someone who says he's a friend.

THE LATIN DREAM OF GRANDMOTHERS

All the grandmothers sail tonight in a ship
toward the true flat edge of the earth.
They will dock and begin their lives again,
choose lovers Argentinian and taste
the sheer red meat of roses in their teeth.
None of us will be born in the next

century. They have taken their old skin,
webs of invisible light and mouths crimped
like old petunias, wind curled in jam jars,
a long braid. For days they have swept the decks
with no sleep no sleep and now land rinses
them hot with its black breath, torches ruffling

red on shore. At last a little luck:
The wind has teased them backward like
tongues. When they step down they will be thanking
memory for being stronger than a world,
be dancing *viña roja* in the arms
of poets, revolutionary men.

Their breasts will sit up again, their hips say
and say. Tonight even my grandmother
leaves off pissing the floor and forgetting,
sails away with her bones to listen
to guitars, the foreigners she never
trusted. *Esta noche* she believes means the sea

is violet. Tonight even yours lets
history down in her skirt. A young lover
sings. A flute feathers her ear. Soon it will
be all silence, here in this century,
there; where the moonlight's warm buzz
strings a word, a heart, *un corazon.*

OLD COUNTRIES

for Dick

Last night your father was tired and sang
the old Russian song, *Sing, little songbird,*
sing. You are a dumb son of a bitch.

Early, before light, you lay awake
wondering why he never told you before
about his cousin from Lithuania
who taught him to sing, about the grandfather
who won the lottery and bought a horse
that had cancer and died. Rivka, your grandmother
with the heavy eyebrows, kept all the money
after that. You try to picture the man you met
only once, when you went with him
to get a pack of Chesterfields
and he bought you a little boat.

You can never find them
because they changed their names
when they came over on the ship.
As the story goes, your name
came from the man ahead of them,
a peddler from East London.

But then there's Uncle Chanya's tale
that your grandmother was never sent for
from the old country, and came anyway
on her own, and found her husband
with a sick race horse. She believed in names.
She could find the one wolf
in all New York: Your grandfather,
the pin peddler, whose name was Bill.

Your father couldn't explain how she found him,
not if the story of the name was true.
And if it was not, how did she know the people
would still be there where the names
had left them? So he says there is another story

that the relatives in the old country
got sick of her, a manless woman,
a wigmaker's daughter, no good to matchmakers.
Useless, they said, useless as a hat
on a dog. In those days the country, he said
was full of fools and dogs

but they had a logic about leaving.
Someone would start talking of a place
where you could get rich, eat meat
on weekdays. *Hock mir a chinik,*
the others would say.

But your grandmother came, and later
your father's cousin who taught him
the old song. And she told him a story
that she had a first name
but that it had changed
when she nearly died of diphtheria at ten.
No one remembers it.

Last night when your father was tired
he told you the same old story:
That his father had come from there
and bought a horse. Its sides
began to crease with bone,
its eyes began to ring
with delicate concave shadows.
After six years he had written his wife,
sent her part of the money, saying
there was more. Your father was not born yet.

But there was a child
who had died in the old country
whom they never spoke about. That was how
she knew how to find him.
Uncle Chanya claimed her at the dock
because your grandfather had some business
in the country. With a carrot he led
the little gray ridge of horse out in the snow
and shot it.

The horse's name was Malkeh.

GENERATION

In a dream the eye swallows the body.
A son takes his father to get new glasses
and buys him a watch. The father says,
The doctor was a quack; these are no good
and I can't see the numbers on the watch.
The son returns the watch and makes an appointment
with a new optometrist. His father calls
in the middle of the night screaming,
What time is it? What do you do for me?
I'm all alone. In a dream the ear

floats above the body like an undiscovered
moon. The son drives over to the house
in his pajamas. His father sits in moonlight
writing his will and muttering, There's nothing
to eat. The windows are dark even in the dream's
perfect night vision. Leopards are strolling
the lawn, so quiet in their step the son hears
their throats which sound like someone in bed
eating lettuce. Shoot me one of those leopards,

his father says, then I'll eat. The son finds
an old archery set in a closet and wanders
back to the grass. Leopards wind around
palm trees and roses in the moonlight. Such
is the magnetism of vegetables in dreams.
The leopards look at him brilliantly
as if he's doing something for them
standing there in his pajamas with his handful
of arrows. Secretly, he tunes in their casual

conversation about the grass and the lovely
tickle of insects about their loins. He drops
the arrows. His father's head swells up

like a huge boil in the front window.
What's wrong with you, he howls, you fool,
you son of a bitch. What do you do for me?
But the son is watching leopards curl to sleep
on the chimney and beneath the Buick, their whole
bodies painted like eyes. My, my, he says
as the sun flapjacks some red on the roof
and parked cars along the street loll
and glow like they've been ravished, My, my.
Just look at the time.

BIRDSCAPING

In ten years this will be your view:
the moss
will etch to a close,
the red fray
in the bark of a sycamore
where a woodpecker lifted
small beetles on its tongue.
Slowly,
the space in the trees will fall
to a place on the water—
their yesterday.

The secret of hedgerows
and vines is their casual look
that takes time. Choose juniper
or blackhaw which attracts
forty-five species, spills

a fruit raving with ants,
a clean seed
by autumn; a crack
the worms hear. This

can be yours. A harmony
of prey
like fingers after music, music
after air or what
neighbors will think
is the sound of someone
learning another language—

that nervous shift from ground to air.
In memory

there is a height
to sequence. Migrations
are always a bursting
of buried geography: After the leaves
the snow. Before the snow
sky

and the square chances
of lawns, risk
of windows, the fuchsia
slitting its own throat.

The scene you want
is here: the orange tree subtle
to the tree it will become, leaning its warm
fruit against shadows now
lost as music.

What's wrong with our gardens
is that everything shows evidence
of our hands.
If you let what the green forgets
be landscape, the seasons
come together.

Tomorrow roots will cut the earth
and hawthorn will catch
and all you have to do is wait,
let the trees hold air
as if both of you
had planned for everything.
Closed-winged, the tanager,
the jay,
will float down. The sore

in the rose where the aphids
have sifted, the beetle
spinning in a pool, the pod's
eyelid removed,
will draw them. Their shadows
will become what the grass thinks,
and in the window
the veil your body makes
will not print, but remain
what they fly through.

L'AGE MÛR

Camille Claudel, 1864–1942

When the air got in the room with me
and the chair, the air was the oblong room
it ran along, picking up windows
which climbed inside it. Morning.
Two figures parted, and hers was reaching a moment
in the concave space his had withdrawn from. He
stole everything. Even this.
The snow at Ville-Evrard clung like a plaster, aware
of nothing going on outside it.

The wild boar Rodin returns home
and the cat is waiting in the bushes. So the gossips
said. Then there was the war.

In Montdevergues after that the doctors
had a saying, We begin
by killing; we end by healing.
But I don't know goodbye from hello.
I mold a head of Bismarck, of Napoleon, the light
brimming with consideration, and Dubois says,
"Have you worked with Monsieur Rodin?"
Of the dream that was my life
this is the nightmare.

The way the old woman in the bronze
is about to pull him
through her; the way I once felt my breasts,
two mutes, arrive beneath my hands. The sixth sense
of my back. Space scented me; it hesitated
and I saw it pass. But thought
for a moment of the pain
of a mother who never forgives you
for a wrong you cannot remember.
The bowed air between two nudes meeting
or parting, as human as this.

SPRING

Outside, the mouths of your horses tear
down to the white of the grass.
The cottonwoods end.
Day drops with the clean sweat
of candles. In the room men are clouding
your death with flesh, murmuring
about the hairlike quality of your hair; how strange
finding the bruised gray couch without you.

All around me the small vibrations
of your name pass from lip to lip
while in the kitchen the tops of cakes
wrinkle, grow cool
and the young priest like a beautiful
black tent
sits in the wind of the oven.

A light square rests in the wallpaper
where a mirror was removed this morning.
Young colts are understanding
the swirled face of water
in the tin trough
behind the house.

Dusk releases every shape. Cut flowers
catch in the windows.
Your cool fingers reach out
and print the air as though it were a goblet.
Grief is the second life. The priest's skirt
pours over and over again like wine.

IV

WALKING IN THE SOLSTICE

Tonight no one makes love. Genie silhouettes
of women float, their B-movie negligees skimming screens
among the motels half-lit and wholly quiet.
Suddenly I am the stranger following cigarettes
down avenues in the innocence of suburbs, the cat
who walks with the warp of evening mist through parking lots
and elm frazzle to lie in the toy tropic of lawns.

I don't take anyone with me, not even to hear
the radios throw thistles of Sinatra, Tormé.
Nothing I'd do would make one bed groan
under the moon-dumped roofs, or move the young men whose
mouths lie tented under newspapers. Tonight they don't
hear the junk rain of car keys, or gun for curves.
There is time to learn by heart along the way
the sudden graveyard
of the drive-in, the lunar funk of a living room
where a man sets his dinner tray before
John Wayne. A girl in a second story undresses

to the eunuch in the mirror. No complaints.
Just for tonight the need goes away. It is all
in perspective: The housewife is dreaming of Aristotle,
the salesman lying down with his shoes. And the sulfurous
green-blue of the night horizon
is crowded with blacknesses like boats.

STATE STREET MOTEL

The wallpaper is full of larkspurs
which halve and curl at each seam. You lie on the bed.
The mirror holds a precise dark mouth
where the tip of the closet door is open.
I am watching you and thinking
how we took a train to get here
through snow, the tiny curtains that parted
New Haven, White River, Montpelier Junction.
It was two hours late and then somewhere
outside a town, swelled to a stop.
The lights blotted off
the shapes of passengers' heads
all along the car, the crackle
of someone stepping on a candy wrapper. Inside
our window, a birch's comb, glazed,
and the snow's seals, broken and pasted back
over footprints. Everyone whispered. But now
there's nothing louder than two suitcases
set neatly in a corner of this room, a day

where snow on the hills lifts like thin paper.
I am writing this down because I don't understand
anything about us. In this room, a bed, a blanket
flipped over like a leaf of a calendar:
In April there's always a picture of a meadow,
a quote from Wordsworth, a holiday
for fools. Your curled hand is emptying exhausted ponies
from the edge of the bed
onto the hard yellow carpet. I'm here
watching you sleep because six years ago
we promised each other something.
We were married outdoors. I can't remember
the last time I stayed awake this long.
The snow outside you falls,

light the January sky tears up. What is this place?
When do we arrive? Maybe
the dreams that keep us going
are no better than our lives.

Maybe it hasn't turned out like this.

REFRACTION

1.

One spring he was loved
because he could repeat sequences
of up to nine numbers, backwards:
A split second response
as if the numbers were leaves, and he
their shadows.

It was that close.
They kept him for hours; April
light slathered on the laboratory windows
like some new golden age.
And, for a while, he came back
spilling phone numbers and addresses
from the third story window
where he could see the knobby tips
of plum trees, and college women strolling
into clusters. And he calculated

the dust-soft expansions
and warp of a model universe.
Had taken, on returning from Saigon,
thirteen successive photographs
of the Golden Gate Bridge at dusk

and worked construction for a summer,
teaching himself the language houses
and bridges speak. It was that easy

to disappear and not write.
Those who loved him will imagine
he is living some kind of life
like the one just off the border
of his last Hawaiian postcard—

as if the years were those frozen
peacock-stiff waves just rolling in
and he, their breaking

off this coast,
glimmering, and never out of order.

2.

But order is small. His ex-wife shows up
with his old Christmas ornaments,
nervous and drunk. Up to her chin
with little cardboard trays
of painted aluminum pine cones, hot pink,
green, cadillac blue with silver flecks
showing through. It is August. "Here,
I thought you should have these," she says.

We listen to jazz, progressive, drink gin
and tonic. She confesses she's tired of showing Annie
his picture and saying, *that's Daddy.*
On his birthday,

no one speaks. He used to stand up
and say *God bless America* when he was drunk.
I've got some of his old letters/ *All the hills
in Nam have numbers/ Merry Christmas, P. S. Can you
send dollars.*

There's always a certain correspondence
between a man and his absence. "My luck," she whispers,
"I marry a dreamer; they tell him he's a genius."
In the world's stupid proportions, all women
believe men are dreamers and geniuses
and all the men believe it. Think of his poor daughter
raised on a grin in a photograph, a perfectly
repeated idea. It's enough

to make us sit till evening, unrelated
except to the lawn chairs and the yard.
Night hovers on fences, phone wires, leaf points,
reversing everything gradually. Black. She says,
"I can think of a hundred times when we
used to sit out like this," her face
assembling slowly in the last flood of light. The straw
looks broken where it enters
gin in her glass.

DESERT WINTER

The rain continues where it left off
last time. The glass gets fever cold.
Otherwise, it's only a subtle change in the light
over days, from a full bliss
to a remembered one, from front room
to hallway. Nightly the same helicopter swoons
its long cone of light into the bleached lawns,
the secret diagrams of patio chairs. Maybe
it's the police archangeling this town, looking
for trouble and catching only the unnatural
white grapefruit, the lilac veins of air
like night with its eyelid turned back.

No real question that this
is not real suffering like the houses
that go snowblind in Helena,
Montana, or my brother's voice calling
long-distance from Thanksgiving ice
in Massachusetts wondering why, at 44, he
the undisputed King of Plastics,
Master of Talking Cops Out of Tickets,
is losing the heart of his wife.

I go about my business; he about his.
He says, *You know me.*
You could drop me naked in the snow
in Denver and I'd have a bottle, a warm bed
and a hot woman within 48 hours.
But this winter, he says,
the whole climate of the earth is gone haywire.
In a few thousand years the desert
will be a French bedroom of ice.
Even now the nights
grow longer. A chopper drags
the last white spire of geometry away.

BALCONIES

It has been an odd life. The mortgage payments figured
according to my weight. The naked flights alongside
the windows of classrooms where children glimpse me
through their taped-up paper snowflakes. The cars I've
flown off cliffs. I wake up at thirty-four, confused.
I don't know if I'm broke or just sexy. August crickets
cha-cha their change. But the house, the house is deep
as fur, and the pillows hold petals of bourbon.
Next door a man is stopped by wild deer in his dreams.
He could lick the hush of late summer. Late night.
Far off, the lonely groundskeeper slants his mower
where willows ellipse the eighth green. Lately
I have been thrown from balconies by lovers
I do not know. I bounce on the velvet of the dark.
Sometimes I eat plums and cold chicken. Sometimes I sit
and let the television flicker the floor
until it offers me diamonds for only ten dollars.

THE WRITING LIFE

You get up in the morning. Sometimes.
And you remind yourself you'd like to catch
this light a moment earlier, the second before
you're looking and figuring how you can use it:
Maybe the unraveling ghost cones of dust,
the magnification of the linden branch, its dark
islands moving across your floor like the glances
of shy girls.

Last night a multimillionaire on t.v.
told you six ways to get rich right now
in America, with no capital. You took no notes,
knew you wouldn't understand because you're broke
right now in America with no damn words
coming. Nothing in your head like the z
on the typewriter that won't print.
How you love this life. You begin, today,

remembering, once, in Italy, you chewed
a coffee bean that was floating in your liqueur.
You write about the taste of it. You hope
in its deep bitterness a love story
about tourists and cultural contradictions
will burst. By noon, you have a table
and the man's name. *Armando.* No, too Spanish.
Fabrizio. Good work.

At four it occurs to you one germ, one itch
of a finger at the switch could do it. That's
the goddam problem. At five, the universe
expands—not measurably, but nevertheless
tragically, if you're sensitive. Your son
will grow up to hate you. You need a drink.

At night Fabrizio walks to the Piazza Esedra,
sits in the cafe and smokes. The church behind him,
he tells the tourists all week, is
the last thing Michelangelo ever did.
The young boys are walking now under the lindens
looking for a man to take them home.
He thinks in all things hesitation
is the most beautiful. He thinks he knows
the last thing Michelangelo
really would have done. And this

is enough for Fabrizio; you lean back,
the house if quiet and you sneak
to the window with a smoke. It makes you
dizzy and glad while you're dying anyway.
Tonight, the distant cars swell importantly
into the silence, like your thoughts
when others sleep. Write this down

or you'll lose it. Tomorrow, the woman
for Fabrizio will arrive, rich, from America.
Somehow they'll meet. You'll find the words
because the sadness has come already
in the streets by the cafe, and the fiction
cannot help them any more than the fact
of light. The dog is dreaming.
The grass is wet. The evangelist on t.v.
sweats like Christ. Someday these things
scrawled quickly in the heart will matter
and you'll pause one lovely, lonesome second
before you turn, and say them right.

KEEPING WARM IN NEW YORK

That morning, Sunday morning, was clearer.
The avenue sharpened; nothing open
while we waited for a hotel room, hunted
coffee. You grew up
in this cold, you said, but now
there was nothing left in your body
that could remember well enough
to keep it out. Sometimes, waiting for a bus,
you used to pray. We keep walking,
clutching ourselves as if suddenly
we really shudder out of love and are not
ashamed. And we try the door of a church,

enter cautiously, slide into a back pew, let
our palms open. The nave is empty and warm
like the space where someone has just slept.
Church of the Incarnation, you whisper, *oh God,*
we're just a couple of frozen Jews.
The flowers on the distant altar blush
at us. Gladiolas tall as my arms.
It is before the service, and the wiry sexton
paces the front aisles like an abandoned groom.
The carnation in his lapel makes another face,
white as surprise. Everything suspects us.

Later we pass the delicatessen
where you ate the rehearsal dinner
before your first wedding, one August
in the fifties. Inside, a few old men
lean on their elbows and are still talking.
That afternoon a black voice hisses
through the wall by our bed, *If you ain't here*
in eight minutes I'm gonna kill you motherfucker.
We are tired and warm and the snow

shadow-showing behind the sheer curtains
of our seventh floor window
touches and touches itself
on the way down. We hear a knock. His voice
snarling, *Who is it?*
Her voice, softly, *Me.*
And we sleep.

FABLE: THE WOMAN AND THE IRIS

But this is no
mere gossip: this is the sack
when the knife is still,
the body foxy with its change
of heart. I know a woman who fell
in love with a voice. And at the end
of this voice dangled a man
like moon cheese. She sent him
an iris. An anonymous note.
Though it's true of men in love
that they cannot read.

And so this man all his life has been
merely dreaming her out of himself—seeing
in the bloom's minute white ovaries
and bashful instruments
of joy, waiting to be called

toward the body where the sack is lost,
the hands blue. A woman is left to explain
to her nieces that this is all right—
this is how far away love stands,
as far as wine from milk.

Think then of this passing bowl
of memory, robbed of all its thickness,
as what she has—what the lovers
huddled in history,
blind as potatoes in a sack,
must smell inside.
The woman and the man
with her flimsy iris one day

go to the mountains of Nevada
or a lake. A lake bird squeaks at them:
This is the alphabet with only o
and v. I do not know what happened then; how
once we have loved
we are never born again. I know
a real woman can fall

into anything like Gretel into a trap.
But the flower—
it can't even imagine a shape
that is not a flower . . .

FIRST LOVE

At night we'd haunt the bleachers' back row. Out there
was the center of something, baldness
quietly taking hold in the grass. Moths against
the stadium light like torn up notes.
When the traffic died some nightbirds
stuck in citrus along MacDonald Avenue
would whistle once at the silence, something
you forget nightbirds ever do, until they do.

I'd heard a story once about a flyball gone foul
and denting in the dark blue roof of someone's Pontiac
parked in the lot of Queen of Peace Church.
I used to wonder if a person could be killed
that way, walking casually toward downtown
by the right field fence.

In 1971, love was like that,
falling where the body was and where
the wind carried: though he was short
and asthmatic. I stood there like one of the Mexican kids
on car bumpers waiting for some hard swing to send one
over, hollering, *This one's mine*. And then
they'd scramble and elbow one another for it
like the whole safety of the free world
depended on this. But at night they were gone

and it was different, hollow, and he'd sit
a long time without speaking. I'd wait a long time
for something I believed he was going to say.
Once I put my hand
inside his shirt, feeling the strange cloudiness of hair.
Spring air from the field sank

like cooled coffee, a stone in shade.
I remember thinking I'd remember this
and it would come to me later on its own

when I'd just be walking casually at night
to lock the back door, or sitting down
to write a letter, deciding to whom . . .

HORSES AT ESTERO BEACH

Tonight I want to believe they're still
waiting on the uneven sand and staring
out onto, or over, the blue abstraction
of ocean. And some of them
with the mattered eyes flies love, and some
showing like old brass in the sun
and beside them the Mexican boy with his open shirt
hoping we will change our minds
and be the day's first customers. But we only look

and imagine the movies—
I remember Brando on his way, riding
to see the sheriff's Mexican daughter.
You remember Becket and the King
shouting above the cold English coast.
And they will always ride like that, as long
as there are waves

and late night television, washing
the bed with silver
like an old love we can still see
but from a distance
and in a sadder light. Then, we just kept moving

toward the crippled edge of the bay,
carrying our shoes, jeans rolled up
on our white legs. And everywhere our feet
pressed on the wet sand, small ashen auras
spread and vanished. I guess neither of us
felt like being in the movies, caught
in the soft frames of the wind
because we said nothing. We stood
by the ocean looking back
at the desolate patios of the hotel,
the air the color of wet paper
above the violet open lips of bougainvillea.

That night you put warm wet towels
on my puffed stomach where our child
used to be. And we didn't close the curtains
but watched the moonlight
and someone crazy sat out on the pier
trying to fish. And others came back late
turning their keys and laughing
and dropped their shoes.

Then I listened to your breathing
so I wouldn't hear my own.
I was planning to dream of those horses
moving slowly as the boy led them home.
I don't remember if I did.
But I think of them often,
their curved bellies, their smooth flanks, and ribs
molded over their bodies like sand
on sand.

Tonight I want to tell you they're out there
shapely and dark with waiting
and it would have been so easy
though, by now, I think the boy knows
we're walking under the shade of the cabanas
and up the steps, receding, and we're never
coming back. The mares are watching
the last scene in the world, sand and water,
as if it's an empty screen. Maybe
they lie down slowly and breathe.

As if the sky were a warm damp towel
growing cool.

THE CLOUD BY DESIRE

It is day in the movie,
night here,
and they have submarined north
testing

invisible fallout. It is days after
the end of the visible world.
Already ghosts

these men underwater, pale
as the screen's daylight
projecting on us, tones and shapes

of San Francisco Bay.
The periscope reads
its blank docks, still streets—
one crewman's home town,
so he has to have a look.

Through the hatch he escapes
for shore, and they are calling to him:
God's Gregory Peck voice
through the surfaced megaphone
calling to him who wants
to die at home.

When the captain dreams it is daylight
it's never here, but north
where he was born. Though he's
never returned, the barns

are still pitched, the gas cans
oxblood with rust. The cows
in winter

with saliva freezing
on their muzzles, melting
with their next breath . . .

Place has its advantage over them
like the body. No one's
content to end
in the Mexican cancer clinic,
the Swiss miracle spa.
When they finally give up
it's for home.

That's why
these sailors return to harbor
and, when the sickness comes,
forget their last moment love affairs
and go north again
to nothing

but the idea of nearness:
There is a field of corncribs
and a silo. A bridge. Sky
with its tangerine streak.
The grocery stores

are open. The horse standing,
the grass moving. A cloud
by desire.

And day there . . . night here.